PROJECT MANAGEMENT

BOOK

OF
TEMPLATES

NAVAID UR REHMAN ,MS,PMP

ABOUT THE AUTHOR

Rehman is the Senior Project Manager and former Assistant Professor at Engineering University, with over 20 years of professional consulting and academic experience across Canada, the Middle East (UAE), and other countries.

He graduated in Civil Engineering with specialization in Project Management from the University of Alberta, Canada. He is a certified Project Management Professional (PMP) ® and Certified ISO Lead Auditor. He is a Subject Matter Expert in Project Management (Fundamental & Advanced), and created PMO and Project management tools.

ABOUT THE BOOK

This project management book provides a sequence of templates and checklists required to execute the project under project management process groups, i.e., Initiation, Planning, Execution, Monitoring & Control, and Closing.

This book aligns with PMI's PMBOK® and covers all project management process groups.

Templates and checklists are flexible, concise, and comprehensive to use in different types of projects.

Templates are designed to facilitate project managers for getting the job done in a systematic way within the time frame and project budget.

Copyright © 2021 by Navaid Ur Rehman

ISBN: 9798719847344

TABLE OF CONTENTS

CHAPTER 4 – MONITORING & CONTROL PROCESS   146

CHAPTER 5 - CLOSING PROCESS   174

CHAPTER 1
INITIATION PROCESS

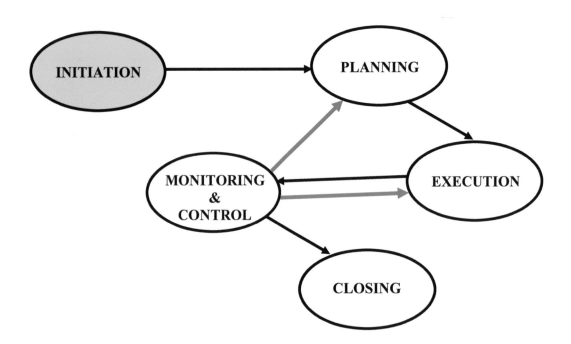

Initiation is the process of **defining and authorizing** the **start** of a new project or a new phase of a project.

PROJECT MANAGEMENT

INITIATION

LIST OF TEMPLATES AND FORMS

1. Project Charter

2. Stakeholder Management

3. Contract Review

4. Project Library

PROJECT MANAGEMENT

PROJECT CHARTER

Project Charter is the document that formally authorises and approves the project and documenting the initial key project information that satisfy stakeholder's needs and expectations.

TEMPLATE SUPPORT

Project Sponsor:

Person from higher management who acts as an owner of the project in the company and is accountable for project success and failure.

Project Objective:

Plan to achieve by the end of the project. Project objective categories: Quality, Cost, Time, Safety, Business, Performance, Technology, etc.

Contract Type:

Fixed-price contract, Cost-reimbursable contract, Time & Material Contract

Project Capital Value:

Overall cost that may associate with land acquisition, planning, design, permitting, construction, development, construction supervision, material, equipment.

Consultancy Contract Fees:

Fees for services to be carried out as per contract.

Consultancy Man Hours:

Calculate Man Hours for services to be carried out either based on the average Man-Hour rate or team members' individual rates.

Performance Security Bond:

Performance bond is the security against the failure to meet the contractual obligations. Performance bond shall be released after the service is completed successfully. Performance bond value shall be % of Consultancy contract value. This value is provided by the client in the contract.

Penalties /
Liquidated Damages:

Penalties/Liquidated Damages refer to delay penalty on the project. Delay Penalty value shall be % of Consultancy contract value. This value is provided by the client in the contract.

Direct Liability/
Indirect or Consequential Damages:

It is a legal obligation of the company for any negligence resulting any injury or property damage to the client. These liabilities or losses are covered through insurance. Liability limit is provided by the client in the contract.

Project Duration:

Total time given by the client to complete the project

Project Schedule /Milestones:

Write the planned submission dates of deliverables and milestones.
Refer to the Project Schedule template in process group. Detailed project schedule provides the planned or forecast date for activities.

Project Engineering & Management Team:

Refer to Organizational Breakdown Structure template in planning process group.

Project Warranty Period:

Warranty period refers to the phase after completion of the project to fix the snags or defects. Warranty period is provided by client in the contract.

Project Scope of Services:

Study, Feasibility, Design, Design Review, Development, Testing, Commissioning, Construction, Supervision.

Project Boundaries:

Set the project scope boundaries and freeze the scope and approve by the client.

Project Opportunities:

Project opportunity is the risk that is a positive event.

Examples:

- Change in Local or Federal Government policies
- New technology
- Additional resources available
- Priority project for the company
- Completion of project before time
- Completion of project under budget

Project Threats:

Project Threat is the risk that is a negative event.

Examples:

- Unavailability of resources
- Non-availability of expertise
- Tight schedule/duration constraint
- Limited budget
- Less priority project for the company
- Approvals delay
- Delay in sub-contract work

Project KPIs

Main Project KPIs are Schedule, Quality, Budget, Team Performance, and Project Effectiveness.

Project KPIs should be SMART (Specific, Measurable, Attainable, Realistic, and Time-bound).

Project Expected Result:

- Project is Fit-For-Purpose
- Meets client expectations
- Project complete within budget and time requirements

Project Title	
Project Sponsor	
Client	
Project Objectives	
Client Expectations	
Client Tender No	
Contract Award Reference & Date	
Company Internal Project No.	
Contract Type	
Project Capital Value	

Consultancy Contract Fees	
Contract Man Hours	
Client Project Manager	
Company Project Manager	
Performance Security Bond	
Penalties /Liquidated Damages	
Direct Liability/ Indirect or Consequential Damages	
Project Duration	
Project Schedule /Milestones	

Project Management Team	Nos.	Name	Role	Responsibilities

Project Engineering Team	Nos	Discipline	Name	Role	Responsibilities

Project Warranty Period	
Project Start Date	
Project End Date	
Project Scope of Services	
Project Boundaries	

Project Opportunities	Short term: Long term:
Project Threats	
Project KPIs	
Project Expected Result	

PROJECT MANAGEMENT

STAKEHOLDER MANAGEMENT

Stakeholder identification and analysis is the process to identify the people or organization who can directly or indirectly influence the project, and it can have a negative or positive impact on the project.

TEMPLATE SUPPORT

Project Internal Stakeholders:

- Project team from multidiscipline
- Support Department
  - ☐ Management
  - ☐ Business Development
  - ☐ Human Resource
  - ☐ Finance
  - ☐ Procurement
  - ☐ Legal
  - ☐ IT
  - ☐ HSEQ

Project External Stakeholders:

- Client
- Government Authorities or Regulators
- Consultants
- Vendors
- Suppliers
- Contractors
- Sub-Contractors
- Financial Institution (Banks, Insurance Companies)
- Associations
- NGOs

PROJECT INTERNAL STAKEHOLDERS (PROJECT TEAM)				
Nos.	Discipline	Name	Role	Responsibilities

PROJECT INTERNAL STAKEHOLDERS (SUPPORT DEPARTMENTS)				
Finance, Procurement, HR, Business Development, etc.				
Nos.	Department	Name	Role	Responsibilities

	PROJECT EXTERNAL STAKEHOLDERS				
Nos.	Local Government Authority	Primary Stakeholders	Secondary Stakeholders	Role	Contact Information

STAKEHOLDER ANALYSIS

EXTERNAL STAKEHOLDERS

No.	Stakeholders	Description	Need & Interest	Primary Secondary Impact	Remarks	Significant Influence	Some Influence	Little Influence	No Influence
						Significant Importance			
						Some Importance			
						Little Importance			
						No Importance			

INTERNAL STAKEHOLDERS

No.	Stakeholders	Description	Need & Interest	Primary Secondary Impact	Remarks	Significant Influence	Some Influence	Little Influence	No Influence
						Significant Importance			
						Some Importance			
						Little Importance			
						No Importance			

Primary Stakeholder (P)	Main
Secondary Stakeholder (S)	Not directly involved
Impact	High (H)
	Medium (M
	Low (L)

PROJECT MANAGEMENT

CONTRACT REVIEW

Contract Review is the process of examining the document for its accuracy and correctness, finding out the deviations from the Request for Proposal (RFP) and analysing the impact of deviation, and providing acceptance criteria for deviations.

TEMPLATE SUPPORT

Request for Proposal:

Company prepares and submits the proposal based on the document received from the client during the bidding stage. The RFP specifies client requirement. It includes Project scope, duration, contractual conditions, information to bidders, and evaluation criteria.

Contract Agreement:

Contract agreement is a legal document. It is an agreement between the client and the company who will carry out the services. Once the project is awarded, RFP including all addendums and clarifications becomes the Contract document.

Deviation:

Review the contract agreement and compare with Request for Proposal (RFP). Find out the deviations if there are any changes in contract agreement.

Impact:

- Cost
- Time
- Quality

Condition of Acceptance:

- Avoid
- Transfer
- Decline
- Accept without qualification or exception

Nos	Description	Request for Proposal (RFP)	Contract Agreement	Deviation	Impact	Acceptance (Yes/No)	Condition of Acceptance
	CONTRACT REVIEW						
1	Scope of the Project						
2	Scope of the Services						
3	Deliverables						
4	Third-Party Scope						
5	Project Location						
6	Project Fees /Price						
7	Advance Fees						
8	Payment Terms						
9	Invoicing Terms						
10	Retention						
11	Project Duration / Schedule						
12	Warranty						
13	Advance Bank Guarantee						
14	Performance Bank Guarantee						
15	Other Guarantees						
16	Insurances						
17	Liabilities						
18	Penalties						
19	Taxes						
20	Safety						

PROJECT MANAGEMENT

PROJECT LIBRARY

Project Library is the database of active and completed projects. This will help to identify the similar projects. A project manager can refer similar projects for lessons learned.

TEMPLATE SUPPORT

Project Type:
_____

- Research
- Study
- Engineering Design
- IT
- Development
- Production
- Manufacturing
- Project Management Consultancy (PMC)
- Construction Management
- Construction Supervision
- Any other

Project Category:
_____

- Oil & Gas
  - Offshore Engineering
  - Onshore Engineering
- Buildings
  - Commercial buildings
  - Residential building
  - Industrial buildings
  - Recreational and Religious buildings
- Infrastructure
  - Infrastructure Land Development
  - Power and Energy
  - Wet Utilities
  - Road & Highways
  - Rail
  - Bridges and Tunnels
- Information Technology
  - Hardware
  - Software
  - Security
  - Services
  - Telecommunication and Networking

- Fire and Safety
- Healthcare
- Chemicals
- Industrial
- Environment

Project Status:

Active
Complete

Project Results:

- Profit
- Loss

PROJECT LIBRARY

Project ID	Project Name	Project Type	Project Category	Client	Award Date	Brief Scope	Project Value	Duration	Location	Project Status	Project Result

CHAPTER 2
PLANNING PROCESS

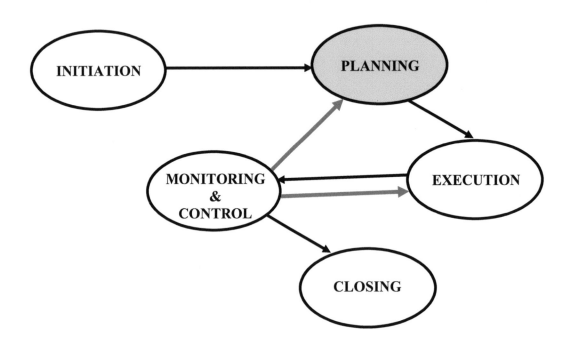

Planning is the process that is necessary to define the **project scope**, refine the **objectives**, and define the action required to achieve the **project's goals**

PROJECT MANAGEMENT

LIST OF TEMPLATES AND FORMS

1. Project Management Checklist

2. Project Management Plan

3. Project Scope Statement

4. WBS Package

5. Activity Log

6. Project Schedule

7. Sample Gantt Chart

8. Project Network Diagram

9. Project Calendar

10. Project Time Sheet

11. Cost Estimate

12. Responsibility Assignment Matrix (RACI)

13. Organization Breakdown Structure (OBS)

14. Project Acceptance Criteria

15. Project Recovery Plan

16. Schedule of Services

17. Scope Responsibility Matrix

PROJECT MANAGEMENT

PROJECT MANAGEMENT CHECKLIST

Project Management Checklist provides step-by-step project activities required to execute the project from beginning to the closeout of the project.

TEMPLATE SUPPORT

Project Phase:

Initiation, Planning, Execution, Monitoring & Control, Closing

Status:

Yes, No, Not Applicable

Targeted Time:

Project Management Checklist activity schedule date

Activity Owner:

Responsible for completion of activity. Team Members, Project Manager, Higher Management, Supporting Departments (PMO Office, Finance, HR, Procurement, etc.)

Date:

Actual project management checklist activity perform date

No.	Project Phase	Project Management Activity Checklist	Status	Targeted Time	Activity Owner	Date
1	Initiation	Contract Review				
2	Initiation	Open Project in system				
3	Initiation	Request for creating Project Home (folder) and request to assign Project Administrator				
4	Initiation	Request for Performance Bond to Finance (if applicable)				
5	Initiation	Request for Advance Payment Bond to Finance (if applicable)				
6	Initiation	Prepare Project Charter				
7	Initiation	Identify Stakeholders and prepare Stakeholder management plan				
8	Initiation	Obtain Project Resources (Team)-Mobilisation				
9	Initiation	External Kick-off Meeting with Client				
10	Initiation	Internal Kick-off Meeting with Project Team and Management				
11	Initiation	Scope Verification				
12	Initiation	Set Project KPIs				

No.	Project Phase	Project Management Activity Checklist	Status	Targeted Time	Activity Owner	Date
13	Initiation	Data Collection				
14	Initiation	Issue Notice of Intent				
15	Planning	Prepare RACI Matrix				
16	Planning	Set Project Communication Protocol & Prepare Communication Management Plan				
17	Planning	Prepare Project Management Plan				
18	Planning	Approval of Project Plan (Internal/external)				
19	Planning	Prepare Baseline Schedule				
20	Planning	Prepare Project Budget				
21	Planning	Prepare List of Deliverables				
22	Planning	Prepare Document Control Register				
23	Planning	Identify Initial Project Risks				
24	Planning	Prepare Risk Register				

No.	Project Phase	Project Management Activity Checklist	Status	Targeted Time	Activity Owner	Date
25	Planning	Prepare Inter-Discipline document squad check				
26	Planning	Prepare Document Control List				
27	Planning	Prepare Project Documents Checker and approver List				
28	Execution	Monthly Progress Report (External)				
29	Execution	Weekly/Bi-weekly Progress Report				
30	Execution	Internal Progress Meeting				
31	Execution	External Progress Meeting				
32	Execution	MOMs (Internal & External meetings)				
33	Execution	Prepare stage-wise Design Reports				
34	Execution	Prepare BOQ & Tender Documents				
35	Execution	Prepare Cost Estimate				
36	Monitoring & Control	Project Design Gate Reviews (at each stage)				

No.	Project Phase	Project Management Activity Checklist	Status	Targeted Time	Activity Owner	Date
37	Monitoring & Control	Review Risk list and update Risk Register (Each Stage of the Project)				
38	Execution	Lesson Learned Sessions (Each Stage of Project)				
39	Monitoring & Control	Project Internal Audit after 50% project completion				
40	Monitoring & Control	Update Project Financial Forecast				
41	Monitoring & Control	Prepare Justification or prepare recovery plan if project slips or creep				
42	Monitoring & Control	Monitor Man Hours & Budget spent				
43	Monitoring & Control	Monitor Project Progress				
44	Monitoring & Control	Evaluate Scope change (if any)				
45	Monitoring & Control	Get approval of scope change from client				
46	Monitoring & Control	Implement only approved changes				
47	Closing	Send CSR (Client Satisfaction Report) to client				
48	Closing	Evaluate CSR with Management				

No.	Project Phase	Project Management Activity Checklist	Status	Targeted Time	Activity Owner	Date
49	Closing	Prepare Closeout Report				
50	Closing	Project Post-Mortem				
51	Closing	Ensure all invoices have been paid				
52	Closing	Complete job completion form				
53	Closing	Request the project closure				
54	Closing	Project Archiving				
55	Finance	Generate Invoices				
56	Finance	Follow up with Finance and Client				

PROJECT MANAGEMENT

PROJECT MANAGEMENT PLAN

Project Management Plan is the guideline for the project team. It sets out the basic principles. These principles shall be used to facilitate smooth performance of the project.

TEMPLATE SUPPORT

Project Directory:

Refer to stakeholder identification and stakeholder analysis document.

Project Team and Responsibilities:

Refer to project organization breakdown structure document.

Project Contractual Data:

Refer to project agreement and contract document.

Project Scope:

Refer to Project Scope Statement, WBS, Third-Party Schedule of Services, Project Assumptions and Exclusions, and Activity log document in planning process group.

Project Acceptance:

Refer to project acceptance criteria document in planning process group.

Project KPIs

Main Project KPIs are Schedule, Quality, Budget, Team Performance, and Project Effectiveness.
Project KPIs should be SMART (Specific, Measurable, Attainable, Realistic, and Time-bound).

Reference Codes, Standards, Specifications:

Refer to project acceptance criteria document in planning process group.

Communication Protocol:

- Delivery Method: hard copy, soft copy, CD, email, fax
- Frequency: weekly, bi-weekly, monthly, one-time, day-to-day basis, as and when required
- Owner: assign team member as an owner of the report, document, or deliverable.
- Audience: documents to be submitted. Audience may be Project Team, Project Manager, Higher Management, Client, Stakeholder, Third-party

Project Completion Criteria:

Refer to project acceptance criteria template in planning process group.

PROJECT MANAGEMENT PLAN

PROJECT INTRODUCTION

- ☐ Project Title
- ☐ Project Number
- ☐ Project Location
- ☐ Project Background
- ☐ Project Objectives

PROJECT DIRECTORY

Key Personnel (Client, Consultant, All Major Stakeholders)

Name	Organization	Position	Role in Project	Telephone	Email

PROJECT TEAM AND RESPONSIBILITIES

Name	Role	Responsibilities

PROJECT CONTRACTUAL INFORMATION

- ☐ Project Duration
- ☐ Project Start Date
- ☐ Project Completion Date
- ☐ Penalties
- ☐ Direct/Indirect liabilities
- ☐ Insurances
- ☐ Security Bonds/Guarantees
- ☐ Governing Law/Court
- ☐ Taxes
- ☐ Payment Terms
- ☐ Invoicing (Financial Milestones /Progress payment)
- ☐ Retention

PROJECT SCOPE

- ☐ Project Scope of Services
- ☐ Project Scope Statement
- ☐ Project Deliverables and Milestones
- ☐ Consultant Scope
- ☐ Third-Party Scope
- ☐ Project Assumptions and Exclusions

PROJECT ACCEPTANCE

- ☐ Project KPIs
- ☐ Project Acceptance Criteria

APPROVALS AND PERMITS

Deliverables	Requirement	Revisions	Client/Authorities

PROJECT DEFINITIONS & ABBREVIATIONS

☐ Definitions
☐ Abbreviations

REFERENCE CODES, STANDARDS, SPECIFICATIONS

☐
☐
☐
☐

COMMUNICATION PROTOCOL

☐ Incoming
☐ Outgoing

COMMUNICATION CRITERIA							
	No.	Description	Detail	Delivery Method	Frequency	Owner	Audience
Reports	1	Monthly Progress Report					
	2	Weekly /Bi Weekly Progress Report					
	3	Management Review Report					
Presentations	1						
	2						
Reviews & Meetings	1	Kick off Meeting					
	2	Internal Kick off Meeting					
	3	Internal Progress Meeting					
	4	Stakeholder Meetings					
	5	Progress Meeting					
	6	Design Reviews					
	7	Project Audit					
Documents & Correspondence	1	E-mail (Informal)					
	2	Verbal					
	3	Fax (Formal)					
	4	Letters (Formal)					
	5	Transmittals (Formal)					
	6	Internal Distribution of Project Documents					
	7	Documents Filing					

PROJECT COMPLETTION CRITERIA

☐
☐
☐
☐

PROJECT MANAGEMENT

PROJECT SCOPE STATEMENT

Project Scope Statement details the project background, defines project boundaries and major milestones and deliverables. It provides the project acceptance criteria based on client's and stakeholders' requirements.

TEMPLATE SUPPORT

Project Boundaries:

Set the project scope boundaries and freeze the scope and approve by the client.

Project Milestones/Deliverables:

Prepare the list of deliverables and approve by the client.

Project Assumptions/Exclusions:

Define the project assumptions and exclusions that are outside the project boundaries.

Project Constraints:

Define the project constraints. That may be Scope, Time, Cost, Quality, Client Satisfaction, and Resources.

Project Acceptance Criteria:

Refer to Project Acceptance criteria document in process group.

Project Title	
Project Background	
Project Boundaries	
Project Deliverables and Milestones	
Project Assumptions and Exclusions	
Project Constraints	
Project Acceptance Criteria	

PROJECT MANAGEMENT

WBS PACKAGE

Work Breakdown Structure (WBS) is the decomposition of the project into deliverables up to smaller elements. Project is easy to plan and execute. Activities are grouped into packages. Project must be divided into logical levels.

TEMPLATE SUPPORT

Work Package:

Group the activities into packages.

Element:

Element is the lowest level (Level 3) where the activity is defined.

Duration:

Provide the duration of each element and deliverable up to Level 0, which will provide you the overall project duration.

Cost:

Provide the cost of each element and deliverable up to Level 0, which will provide you the overall project cost.

WORK BREAKDOWN STRUCTURE				
WBS ID	Work Package	Element Description	Duration	Cost

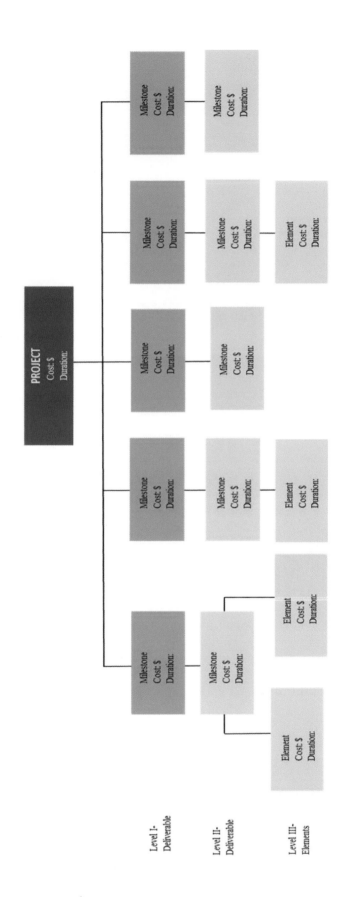

PROJECT MANAGEMENT

ACTIVITY LOG

Activity log provides the activity details, assigning the resources to the activity and the owner of the activity with a unique activity ID.

TEMPLATE SUPPORT

Activity Name:
_____
Refer to WBS to identify the activities.

Resources:
_____
Allocate the resources to each activity to perform.

Owner of the Activity:
_____
Assign the owner of the activity who will be responsible to complete the activity.

Duration:
_____
Assign Activity duration to be completed.

ACTIVITY DEFINITION					
Activity ID	Activity Name	Activity Description	Resources	Owner of the Activity	Duration

PROJECT MANAGEMENT

PROJECT SCHEDULE

Project Schedule assigns the start and end date of milestones and deliverables and measures the progress and delay in the project.

TEMPLATE SUPPORT

Project Phase:

Initiation, Planning, Execution, Monitoring & Control, Closing

Project Tasks /Milestones:

Refer to Activity (Task) log and WBS Package Dictionary in process group.

No of Resources:

No. of resources required to complete activity or task.

Man Hours:

Man Hours required to complete activity or task.

No of Days:

No. of days required to complete activity or task.

Delay:

Activity/Task Delay = Actual days spent to complete the task –Planned days to complete the task

PROJECT SCHEDULE

| Task/Milestone | Project Phase | PLANNED | | | | | | ACTUAL | | | | | | Delay (Days) |
		No. of Resources	Start Date	Finish Date	Man-Hours	No. of Days	No. of Resources	Start Date	Finish Date	Man Hours	No. of Days	

PROJECT MANAGEMENT

GANTT CHART

Gantt Chart is graphical project schedule that provides planning and tracking of activities and tasks. Project Tasks are in sequence with duration.
It provides the project timeline and helps to assign
the resources and delegate the tasks.

TEMPLATE SUPPORT

Sample Gantt Chart:

The basis for this template is House Construction Project. A typical House Construction schedule is provided in Gantt Chart format. This template also provides the basic house construction checklist and systematic activities.

Task Description:

Provide activities in sequence with dependencies.

Activities Dependencies:

Activities Dependencies can be following:

Finish to Start (FS)

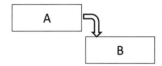
Activity **B** cannot start until Activity **A** finishes

Start to Start (SS)

Activity **B** cannot start until Activity **A** starts

Finish to Finish (FF)

Activity **B** cannot finish until Activity **A** finishes

Start to Finish (SF)

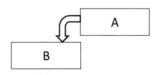
Activity **B** cannot finish until Activity **A** starts

Lead Time:

Lead is a time and duration between successor and predecessor activities. Lead time generally uses a Finish to Start (**FS**) relationship. In other words, these are overlapping activities. Activity **B** can start before Activity **A** finishes.

Example: Activity **A** and Activity **B** has a Finish to Start (**FS**) relationship. Activity **B** starts on 7th January when Activity **A** is near finish and has three (**03**) days left to complete. In this example, Lead time is **3** days, i.e., FS-3days

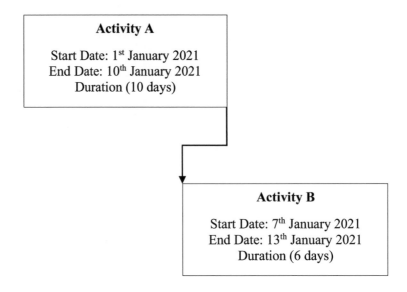

Lag Time

Lag is a time delay of successor activity. Lag time generally is used with all four relationships. Activity **B** can start late after Activity **A** finishes. This delay is called Lag.

Example: Activity **A** and Activity **B** has a Finish to Start (**FS**) relationship. Activity **B** starts on 12th January after Activity **A** finishes on 10th January. In this example, 2 days gap is called Lag, i.e., FS +2 days.

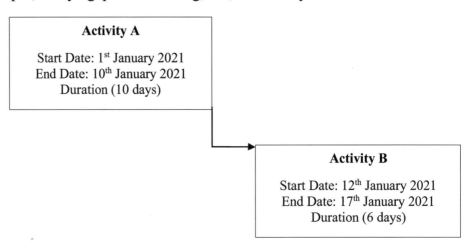

SAMPLE GANTT CHART-HOUSE CONSTRUCTION

Task ID	Task Description	Task Duration	Activity Dependency	Start Date	End Date	No of Days Delay
1	Stakeout Plot	1	Start			
2	Start Excavation	2	FS			
3	Start Deep services	1	SS			
4	Footing	1	FF with Task ID 2			
5	Pour Walls	1	FS			
6	Strip Walls	1	FS			
7	Weeping Tiles	1	FS			
8	Windows Wells	1	FS			
9	Electrical Panel	1	SS			
10	Caping	1	FS			
11	Shallow Services	1	FS			
12	Backfill	1	SS			
13	Ground works	1	FS			
14	Deck Piling	1	SS			
15	Precast Steps	1	FS			
16	Power Meter	1	FS with 2 days lag			
17	Gas Riser	1	SS			
18	Start Framing	8	FS with 4 days lag			

Month-1 (days): 1 2 3 4 5 6 7 8 9 10 11 12 13 14 15 16 17 18 19 20 21 22 23 24 25 26 27 28 29 30

SAMPLE GANTT CHART-HOUSE CONSTRUCTION

Task ID	Task Description	Task Duration	Activity Dependency	Start Date	End Date	No of Days Delay	1	2	3	4	5	6	7	8	9	10	11	12	13	14	15	16	17	18	19	20	21	22	23	24	25	26	27	28	29	30
																											Month-2									
18	Continue Framing	8	FS with 4 days lag						■																										
19	Roofing	2	FS									■																							
20	Fireplace	1	SS									■																								
21	Safety Rail	1	SS									■																								
22	Cabinet Mark out	1	SS									■																								
23	Start Siding	8	FS												■	■	■	■	■	■	■	■												
24	Basement Flooring	1	SS												■																				
25	Garage Flooring	1	SS												■																				
26	Start Plumbing Rough In	4	SS												■	■	■	■																	
27	Order Garage Stairs	1	SS												■																				
28	Heat Rough In	2	FS with Task ID 26															■	■																
29	Electrical Rough In	3	FS																		■	■	■												
30	Rear Deck	2	SS																		■	■													
31	Masonry	1	FS																			■													
32	Structured Rough In	1	FS																				■												
33	Exterior Railing	1	SS																				■												
34	Spray Foam	1	FS																								■								
35	Touch ups	1	SS																								■								
36	Ceiling Poly	1	FS																									■							
37	Frost walls	1	SS																									■							
38	Plumbing Pre-Final	1	FS																										■						
39	Drywall Start	4	FS																											■	■				

SAMPLE GANTT CHART-HOUSE CONSTRUCTION

Task ID	Task Description	Task Duration	Activity Dependency	Start Date	End Date	No of Days Delay	Month-3 (Days 1–31)
39	Continue Drywall	4	FS				
40	Overhead Door	1	FF				
41	Taping	8	FS with Task ID 39				
42	Prime	2	FS				
43	Texture	1	FS				
44	Electrical Rough In	1	FS				
45	Mat Finish	1	FS				
46	Install Mantle	1	SS				
47	1st Stage Finishing	7	FS				
48	Install Cabinets	1	FF				

SAMPLE GANTT CHART-HOUSE CONSTRUCTION

Task ID	Task Description	Task Duration	Activity Dependency	Start Date	End Date	No of Days Delay	1	2	3	4	5	6	7	8	9	10	11	12	13	14	15	16	17	18	19	20	21	22	23	24	25	26	27	28	29	30
																			Month-4																
49	Install Railing	3	FS																																
50	Measure Counter	1	FF																																
51	Paint	5	FS																																
52	Electrical Rough In	1	FS																																
53	Window Clean	1	SS																																
54	Structure Final	1	FS																																
55	Window Lockout	1	SS																																
56	Counter Tops	2	FS																																
57	Tiles	2	FS																																
58	Lino	1	FS																																
59	Hardwood	2	FS																																
60	Stage 2 Finish	1	FS																																
61	Plumb Final	1	FS																																
62	Carpet	2	FS with 1 day lag																																

SAMPLE GANTT CHART-HOUSE CONSTRUCTION

Month-5

Task ID	Task Description	Task Duration	Activity Dependency	Start Date	End Date	No of Days Delay
63	Wire Shelves	1	FS			
64	Mirrors	1	SS			
65	Furnace Clean	1	SS			
66	Heat Final	1	FS			
67	Full Clean	1	SS			
68	Cabinet Final	1	FS			
69	Paint Touch ups (3rd coat)	2	FS			
70	Home Inspection	1	FS			
71	Fix Snag List	2	FS			
72	Construction Complete	1	Milestone			
73	Possession	1	Milestone			

PROJECT MANAGEMENT

PROJECT NETWORK DIAGRAM

Project Network Diagram is schematic and logical representation of the
Project Schedule. It identifies the critical activities
and provides the project duration.

TEMPLATE SUPPORT

Project Network Diagram Representation:

Rectangle box represents an Activity that is called Activity Code. Arrows represent the relationship between predecessor/successor activities. Red arrows show project critical path.

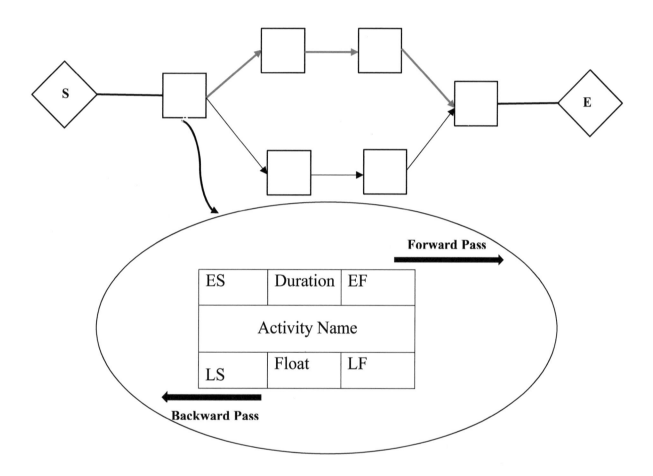

Critical Path:

The critical path is the group of activities or task in sequence that must be the longest path of the project, which provides the shortest possible project duration.

Critical path in sample network is **A, B, D, F** with project duration of 23 days.

Activity Relationship:

Activities relationship can be following:

Finish to Start (FS)

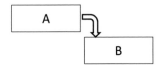

Activity **B** cannot start until Activity **A** finishes

Start to Start (SS)

Activity **B** cannot start until Activity **A** starts

Finish to Finish (FF)

Activity **B** cannot finish until Activity **A** finishes

Start to Finish (SF)

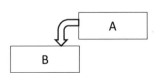

Activity **B** cannot finish until Activity **A** starts

Sample Network Diagram		
Activity	**Relationship**	**Predecessor**
A	Start	-
B	FS	A
C	FS	A
D	FS	B
E	FS	C
F	Finish	D, E

Predecessor activity defines the activity that should complete or start before another activity starts. Successor activity follows the predecessor activity.

Float or Slack:
Float is amount of time that activity can delay.

Free Float: The amount of time that activity can delay without delaying in early start date (ES) of the successor activity.

Total Float: The amount of time that activity can delay without delaying the project end date.

Critical Path Float: Critical path float is always zero "0".

Early Start (ES) & Early Finish (EF):
Early start refers to the earliest date that the activity can start.
Early finish refers to the earliest date that the activity can finish.

Late Start (LS) & Late Finish (LF):
Late start refers the latest date an activity can start without delaying the planned project end date.

Forward Pass and Backward Pass:
Forward pass is a technique to calculate early start (ES) and early finish (EF) dates. The forward pass starts at the beginning of the schedule.
Backward pass is a technique to calculate late start (LS) and late finish (LF) dates. The backward pass starts at the end of the schedule.

Network Diagram Calculation:

◆ Total number of paths in sample network diagram are two.

  1. **A, C, E, F**
  2. **A, B, D, F**

◆ Duration of each path

  1. **A, C, E, F (6+6+4+5 = 21 days)**
  2. **A, B, D, F (6+5+7+5 = 23 days) - Longest path /Critical Path**

  Longest path of the project is **A, B, D, F,** which provides the shortest possible project duration, i.e., 23 days.

◆ Calculation of Early start (ES) and Early Finish (EF)

<u>Forward Pass:</u>

<u>Activity A</u>
ES of Activity **A** starts with **0**
EF = (ES) + (Duration) = 0+6 = **6**

<u>Activity B</u>
ES of Activity B = EF of preceding activity (Activity A is predecessor of Activity B)
ES = **6** (as shown in Activity A calculation)
EF = (ES) + (Duration) = 6+5 = **11**

<u>Activity C</u>
ES of Activity C = EF of preceding activity (Activity A is predecessor of Activity C)
ES = **6** (as shown in Activity A calculation)
EF = (ES) + (Duration) = 6+6 = **12**

<u>Activity D</u>
ES of Activity D = EF of preceding activity (Activity B is predecessor of Activity D)
ES = **11** (as shown in Activity B calculation)
EF = (ES) + (Duration) = 11+7 = **18**

<u>Activity E</u>
ES of Activity E = EF of preceding activity (Activity C is predecessor of Activity E)
ES = **12** (as shown in Activity C calculation)
EF = (ES) + (Duration) = 12+4 = **16**

<u>Activity F</u>
ES of Activity F = EF of preceding activity (Activity D, E are predecessors of Activity F)
ES = (EF) D or EF (E) = 18 or 16 (greater of two) = **18**
EF = (ES) + (Duration) = 18+5 = **23**

◆ Calculation of Late Start (LS) and Late Finish (LF)

<u>Backward Pass:</u>

<u>Activity F</u>
LF of Activity **F** =EF of Activity F = **23**
LS = (LF) - (Duration) = 23-6 = **18**

<u>Activity E</u>
LF of Activity E = LS of Activity F = **18**
LS = (LF) - (Duration) = 18-4 = **14**

<u>Activity D</u>
LF of Activity D = LS of Activity F= **18**
LS = (LF) - (Duration) = 18-7 = **11**

<u>Activity C</u>
LF of Activity C = LS of Activity E= **14**
LS = (LF) - (Duration) = 14-6 = **8**

<u>Activity B</u>
LF of Activity B = LS of Activity D= **11**
LS = (LF) - (Duration) = 11-5 = **6**

<u>Activity A</u>
LF of Activity A = LS of Activity B or LS of Activity C (smaller value)
= 6 or 8 = **6**
LS = (LF) - (Duration) = 6-6 = **0**

SAMPLE NETWORK DIAGRAM

Activity	Relationship	Predecessor	Duration (Days)	Early Start (ES)	Early Finish (EF)	Late Start (LS)	Late Finish (LF)	Total Float =(LS-ES)
A	Start	-	6	0	6	0	6	0
B	FS	A	5	6	11	6	11	0
C	FS	A	6	6	12	8	14	2
D	FS	B	7	11	18	11	18	0
E	FS	C	4	12	16	14	18	2
F	Finish	D,E	5	18	23	18	23	0

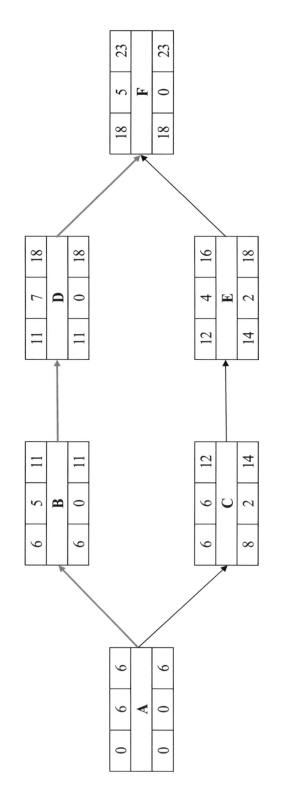

PROJECT MANAGEMENT

PROJECT CALENDAR

Project Calendar is a visual project schedule. It represents the days and dates of the activities to be performed in logical sequence. It also shows the working and non-working days.

TEMPLATE SUPPORT

Sample Project Calendar:
Project: Single-Family House Construction-USA (1500 sq. Ft. to 2200 sq. ft.)
Complete list of house construction activities and duration:

Activity ID	Activity Description	Activity Duration	Activity ID	Activity Description	Activity Duration
1	Stakeout Plot	1	38	Plumbing Pre-Final	1
2	Start Excavation	2	39	Drywall Start	4
3	Start Deep services	1	40	Overhead Door	1
4	Footing	1	41	Taping	8
5	Pour Walls	1	42	Prime	1
6	Strip Walls	1	43	Texture	1
7	Weeping Tiles	1	44	Electrical Rough-in	1
8	Windows Wells	1	45	Mat Finish	1
9	Electrical Panel	1	46	Install Mantle	1
10	Capping	1	47	1st Stage Finishing	7
11	Shallow Services	1	48	Install Cabinets	1
12	Backfill	1	49	Install Railing	3
13	Ground works	1	50	Measure Counter	1
14	Deck Piling	1	51	Paint	5
15	Precast Steps	1	52	Electrical Rough-in	1
16	Power Meter	1	53	Window Clean	1
17	Gas Riser	1	54	Structure Final	1
18	Start Framing	8	55	Window Lockout	1
19	Roofing	2	56	Counter Tops	1
20	Fireplace	1	57	Tiles	2
21	Safety Rail	1	58	Lino	1
22	Cabinet Mark-out	1	59	Hardwood	2
23	Start Siding	8	60	Stage 2 Finish	1
24	Basement Flooring	1	61	Plumb Final	1
25	Garage Flooring	1	62	Carpet	2
26	Start Plumbing Rough-in	3	63	Wire Shelves	1
27	Order Garage Stairs	1	64	Mirrors	1
28	Heat Rough-in	2	65	Furnace Clean	1
29	Electrical Rough-in	3	66	Heat Final	1
30	Rear Deck	2	67	Full Clean	1
31	Masonry	1	68	Cabinet Final	1
32	Structured Rough-in	1	69	Paint Touch-ups-3rd Coat	2
33	Exterior Railing	1	70	Home Inspection	1
34	Spray Foam	1	71	Fix Snag List	2
35	Touch-ups	1	72	Construction Complete	1
36	Ceiling Poly	1	73	Possession	1
37	Frost walls	1			

SAMPLE TASK CALENDAR-HOME CONSTRUCTION

MONTH-1

WEEKS	MONDAY	TUESDAY	WEDNESDAY	THURSDAY	FRIDAY	SATURDAY	SUNDAY
1			1 Start Stakeout Plot	2 Start Excavation Start Deep services	3 Excavation Footings	4	5
2	6 Pour Walls	7 Strip Walls	8 Weeping Tiles	9 Window Wells Electrical Panel	10 Capping	11	12
3	13 Shallow Services Backfill	14 Ground Works Deck Piles	15 Pre-cast step	16	17	18	19
4	20 Power Meter Gas Riser	21	22	23	24	25	26
5	27 Start Framing	28	29	30	31 Continue Framing		

SAMPLE TASK CALENDAR-HOME CONSTRUCTION

MONTH-2

WEEKS	MONDAY	TUESDAY	WEDNESDAY	THURSDAY	FRIDAY	SATURDAY	SUNDAY
6						1	2
7	3 Continue Framing	4	5 End Framing	6 Roofing Fireplace Safety Rail Cabinet Mark-out	7 Roofing	8	9
8	10 Start Siding Basement Flooring Garage Flooring	11 Start Plumbing Rough-in Order Garage Stairs	12	13 End Plumbing Rough-in	14 Continue Siding Heat Rough-in	15	16
9	17 Continue Siding Heat Rough-in	18 Start Electrical Rough-in Rear Deck	19 End Siding Rear Deck	20 End Electrical RI Masonry	21 Structured Rough-in Exterior Railing	22	23
10	24 Spray Foam Touch ups	25 Ceiling Poly Frost walls	26 Plumbing Pre-Final	27 Drywall Start	28	29	

SAMPLE TASK CALENDAR-HOME CONSTRUCTION

MONTH-3

WEEKS	MONDAY	TUESDAY	WEDNESDAY	THURSDAY	FRIDAY	SATURDAY	SUNDAY
11							1
12	2 Continue Drywall / Overhead Door	3 Drywall End	4 Taping Start	5	6 Taping Continues	7	8
13	9 Taping Continues	10	11	12	13 Taping End	14	15
14	16 Prime	17	18 Texture	19 Electrical RI Final	20 Finish Mat	21	22
15	23 1st Stage Finishing Start	24	25	26	27 Install Mantle	28	29
	30 Install Cabinets	31 1st Stage Finishing End					

SAMPLE TASK CALENDAR-HOME CONSTRUCTION

MONTH-4

WEEKS	MONDAY	TUESDAY	WEDNESDAY	THURSDAY	FRIDAY	SATURDAY	SUNDAY
16			1 Install Railing Measure Counter tops	2 Install Railing	3 Install Railing	4	5
17	6 Paint Start	7	8	9	10 Paint End	11	12
18	13 Electrical Final Window Clean	14 Structure Final Window Lockout	15 Counter Tops	16	17 Tiles	18	19
19	20 Tile	21 Lino	22 Hardwood	23 Hardwood	24 Stage 2 Finish	25	26
20	27 Plumb Final	28	29 Carpet	30 Carpet			

SAMPLE TASK CALENDAR-HOME CONSTRUCTION

MONTH-5

WEEKS	MONDAY	TUESDAY	WEDNESDAY	THURSDAY	FRIDAY	SATURDAY	SUNDAY
21					1 Wire Shelves Mirrors Furnace clean	2	3
22	4 Heat Final Full Clean	5 Cabinet Final	6 3rd Paint Coat (Paint Touch up)	7 3rd Paint Coat (Paint Touch-up)	8 Quality Review Home Inspection	9	10
23	11 Fix Snag List	12 Fix Snag List	13	14 Construction Complete	15	16	17
24	18 **Possession**	19	20	21	22	23	24
25	25	26	27	28	29	30	31

PROJECT MANAGEMENT

PROJECT TIMESHEET

Project Timesheet tracks the employees' time spent on the projects and tasks. It provides the basis of recovery of the project and employees' utilization.

TEMPLATE SUPPORT

Recovery:

Recovery = company tied cost factor x utilization factor x productive hours

Company Tied Cost:

Company cost to run the business. Normally consider 65% to 70%
Company Tied Cost Factor = 100/65 = **1.54**

Utilization:

Maximum utilization can be 80% (excluding annual and public holidays).
Utilization factor = 100/utilization (%)

Productive Hours:

Hours booked on projects

Total Hours:

Productive Hours + General Hours (annual holidays, public holidays, booked hours other than project)

Project Cost:

Project Cost = Employee Rate x Productive Hours

PROJECT TIMESHEET							
Employee Name:			Employee No:			Week No:	
Day	Project A	Project B	Project C	Project D	Project E	Public Holiday	Personal Holiday
Monday							
Tuesday							
Wednesday							
Thursday							
Friday							
Saturday							
Sunday							
Productive Hours							
Total Hours							
Employee Rate							
Project Cost							
Recovery							
Utilization							

PROJECT
MANAGEMENT
COST ESTIMATE

Cost Estimate is the document that provides the forecast and actual budget of
the project within a defined and verified scope. This is part of
Project Cost Management Knowledge Area and
Planning Process Group.

TEMPLATE SUPPORT

Project Cost Estimate:

This Template has following sections:

☑ Project Fixed Cost
☑ Project Travelling Cost
☑ Engineering Cost /Resource Account
☑ Project Management Cost / Resource Account
☑ Deployment Schedule of Supervision Staff with Budget
☑ Site Supervision Cost
☑ Third-Party (Sub-Consultant/Sub-Contractor) Services Cost
☑ Material Cost

Project Fixed Costs:

Insurances, Security bonds, Training, Bank Fees, IT Requirements, and any other cost that stays throughout project lifecycle.

Project Traveling Costs:

Applicable to team working virtually from a different city or country.
Applicable if client or project location is different.

Engineering and Project Management Rate and Man Hours:

Proposed rate and man hours refer to planned values whereas actual rate and man hours refer to internal rates (based on employee salary) of the employee and spent many hours on the project.

Resource Account (Employee Cost):

(A) Proposed Cost of the Employee = Proposed Rate x Proposed Man Hours
(B) Actual Cost of the Employee = Actual Rate x Actual Man Hours spent
Variance (Profit/Loss) = **(B)-(A)**

Sample Deployment Schedule with Budget:

- Duration of the project: 12 months
- Cost = Man-Month Rate x Duration

- Monthly Utilization:

  = No. of days worked in a month / Total No. of days in a month
- Cumulative Duration: Month 1 to Month 12
- Cumulative Cost: Man-Month Rate x Cumulative Duration
- Remaining Duration = Planned Duration – Cumulative Duration
- Remaining Cost = Planned Cost – Cumulative Cost

Site Supervision Cost Estimate:

- External Rate: Chargeable rate with client as per agreement or contract.
- Internal Rate: Actual rate calculate based on employee's salary.
- Rate can be calculated on hourly, weekly, and monthly basis. Refer to project timesheet in planning process group.

PROJECT FIXED COST				
Description	Proposed		Actual	
	Unit	Cost	Unit	Cost
Insurances				
Security Bonds				
Bank Fees				
Other Financial Fees				
Production and Printing				
Trainings and Seminars				
Purchasing of Codes and Specifications				
IT Requirement				
Total Fixed Cost				
Variance (Actual Cost – Proposed Cost)				

PROJECT TRAVELING COST				
Description	Proposed		Actual	
	Unit	Cost	Unit	Cost
Car Leasing /Rental				
Air Fair				
Hotel Booking				
Travelling and Daily Allowance				
Visas Cost				
Total Traveling Expenses				
Variance (Actual Cost –Proposed Cost)				

ENGINEERING COST							
Description	Disciplines	Man Hours			Rates		
		Position 1	Position 2	Position 3	Position 1	Position 2	Position 3
Designation							
Proposed	Discipline 1						
Actual							
Proposed	Discipline 2						
Actual							
Proposed	Discipline 3						
Actual							
Proposed	Discipline 4						
Actual							
Proposed	Discipline 5						
Actual							
Proposed	Discipline 6						
Actual							

ENGINEERING RESOURCE ACCOUNT					
POSITION-1		POSITION-2		POSITION-3	
Discipline		Discipline		Discipline	
Designation		Designation		Designation	
Proposed Man Hours (A)		Proposed Man Hours (A)		Proposed Man Hours (A)	
Proposed Rate (B)		Proposed Rate (B)		Proposed Rate (B)	
Proposed Cost C= (AXB)		Proposed Cost C= (AXB)		Proposed Cost C= (AXB)	
Actual Man Hours (D)		Actual Man Hours (D)		Actual Man Hours (D)	
Actual Rate (E)		Actual Rate (E)		Actual Rate (E)	
Actual Cost F= (DXE)		Actual Cost F = (DXE)		Actual Cost F = (DXE)	
Variance (C-F)		Variance (C-F)		Variance (C-F)	

PROJECT MANAGEMENT COST						
	Man-Hours			Rates		
Description	Position 1	Position 2	Position 3	Position 1	Position 2	Position 3
Designation						
Proposed						
Actual						
Proposed						
Actual						
Proposed						
Actual						
Proposed						
Actual						
Proposed						
Actual						
Proposed						
Actual						
Proposed						
Actual						

PROJECT MANAGEMENT RESOURCE ACCOUNT					
POSITION-1		POSITION-2		POSITION-3	
Discipline		Discipline		Discipline	
Designation		Designation		Designation	
Proposed Man Hours (A)		Proposed Man Hours (A)		Proposed Man Hours (A)	
Proposed Rate (B)		Proposed Rate (B)		Proposed Rate (B)	
Proposed Cost C= (AXB)		Proposed Cost C= (AXB)		Proposed Cost C= (AXB)	
Actual Man Hours (D)		Actual Man Hours (D)		Actual Man Hours (D)	
Actual Rate (E)		Actual Rate (E)		Actual Rate (E)	
Actual Cost F= (DXE)		Actual Cost F = (DXE)		Actual Cost F = (DXE)	
Variance (C-F)		Variance (C-F)		Variance (C-F)	

SAMPLE DEPLOYMENT SCHEDULE WITH BUDGET

No.	Specialist/ Personnel Category	Mobilization Date	(A) Planned Duration (Month)	(B) Man-Month Rate ($)	Planned Cost ($) X= (AXB)	1	2	3	4	5	6	7	8	9	10	11	12	(C) Cumulative Duration (M) Sum (1:12)	Cumulative Cost Y=(C X B)	Duration (M) (A-C)	Cost (X-Y)
						\multicolumn{12}{Monthly Utilization 1=100% — 2021}			Project Status		Remaining	
1	Project Manager	01/01/2021	12	25,000	300,000	1	0.8	1	1	1	1	1	1	1	0.75	1	1	11.55	288,750	0.4	11,250
2	Project Engineer	15/01/2021	10	15,000	150,000	0.5	1	1	1	0.9	1	1	1	1	1	1	0	10.40	156,000	-0.4	-6,000
3	Quality Manager	01/02/2021	12	20,000	240,000	0	1	1	1	1	1	1	1	1	1	1	0.7	10.70	214,000	1.3	26,000
4	Cost Engineer	06/06/2021	7	18,000	126,000	0	0	0	0	0	0.83	1	1	1	1	1	1	6.83	123,000	0.2	3,000
5	Planning Engineer	01/01/2021	12	17,000	204,000	1	1	1	1	1	1	1	1	1	1	1	1	12.00	204,000	0.0	0
6	Contract Manager	01/01/2021	8	22,000	176,000	1	1	1	1	0	0	0	0	1	1	1	1	8.00	176,000	0.0	0
																		0.00	0	0.0	0
																		0.00	0	0.0	0
																		0.00	0	0.0	0
																		0.00	0	0.0	0
																		0.00	0	0.0	0
																		0.00	0	0.0	0
																		0.00	0	0.0	0
																		0.00	0	0.0	0
																		0.00	0	0.0	0
																		0.00	0	0.0	0
																		0.00	0	0.0	0
Total			61		1,196,000													59.48	1,161,750	1.5	34,250

| | | | | Actual | | | |
| SITE SUPERVISION COST ESTIMATE | | | | | | | |

Sr. No.	Category (Positions)	Working Days	Monthly Rate (External Rate) X	Actual Rate (Internal Rate /Hour) (A)	Man Hours (B)	Amount C=(AXB)	Variance (X-C)

THIRD-PARTY SERVICES COST				
Third-Party (Sub-Consultant /Contractor)	Scope of Work	Quoted Price (A)	Agreement Price (B)	Savings (B-A)

MATERIAL COST									
			ESTIMATED			ACTUAL			
Nos.	Material	Unit	Unit Cost (A)	Quantity (B)	Estimated Budget C= (AXB)	Unit Cost (D)	Quantity (E)	Actual Budget F= (D X E)	Variance F-C

PROJECT MANAGEMENT

RESPONSIBILITY ASSIGNMENT MATRIX (RACI)

RACI Matrix defines the project team roles and assigns the responsibilities. Roles are assigned for every task and each project management process group.

TEMPLATE SUPPORT

RACI:

Responsibility Assignment Matrix

- Responsible **(R)** Members are persons whose contributions and efforts result in a tangible deliverable or completed task.

- Accountable **(A)** Members are individuals whose approval of the work is required before the task or activity is considered completed.

- Consulted **(C)** Members are persons who play an indirect or advisory role.

- Informed **(I)** Members are persons who should be kept in the loop even though they have no direct or indirect role in the activity.

- Supportive **(S)** Members who support the project team in order to complete a task.

Task \ Role	Role 1	Role 2	Role 3	Role 4	Role 5	Role 6	Role 7	Role 8
PROJECT ROLES & RESPONSIBILITY								
Project Activities	INITIATION							
Task 1	I	I	I	I	I	I	I	I
Task 2	A	I	I	I	I	I	I	I
Task 3	C	C	C	C	C	C	C	C
Task 4	R	C	C	C	C	C	C	C
Project Activities	PLANNING							
Task 1	-	-	-	A	-	-	-	A
Task 2	-	-	-	R	-	-	-	R
Task 3	-	-	-	S	-	-	-	S
Task 4	-	-	-	-	-	-	-	-
Project Activities	EXECUTION							
Task 1	-	-	-	-	A	-	-	-
Task 2	-	-	-	-	R	-	-	-
Task 3	-	-	-	-	S	-	-	-
Task 4	-	-	-	-	-	-	-	-
Project Activities	MONITORING AND CONTROL							
Task 1	-	A	-	-	-	-	-	-
Task 2	-	R	-	-	-	-	-	-
Task 3	-	S	-	-	-	-	-	-
Task 4	-	-	-	-	-	-	-	-
Project Activities	CLOSING							
Task 1	-	A	-	-	-	-	-	-
Task 2	-	R	-	-	-	-	-	-
Task 3	-	S	-	-	-	-	-	-
Task 4	-	-	-	-	-	-	-	-

PROJECT MANAGEMENT

ORGANIZATION BREAKDOWN STRUCTURE (OBS)

OBS is project team structure that formally secures the resources. This defines the team role in the project and their responsibilities. OBS also defines the reporting structure of the team members.

TEMPLATE SUPPORT

Designation:
_____

Official Job Title of the project team member

Role in Project:
_____

Assign the Role to the Team members as per the project requirement.

Responsibilities:
_____

Delegate the Tasks to all project team members.

Reporting to:
_____

Direct line manager of the team member outside the project organization structure.

Level I – Engineering Team:
_____

Lead Engineers of each Discipline

Level II – Engineering Team:
_____

Engineers & Designers reporting to Lead Engineers

ORGANIZATIONAL BREAKDOWN STRUCTURE (OBS) WORKSHEET				
Name	Designation	Role in Project	Responsibilities	Reporting To

ORGANIZATION BREAKDOWN STRUCTURE FOR PROJECT TEAM

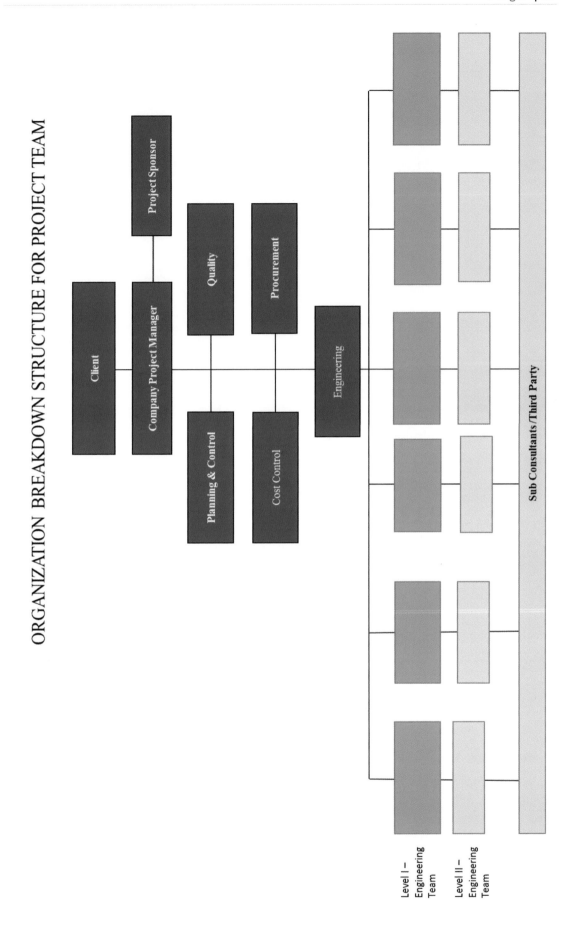

PROJECT MANAGEMENT

PROJECT ACCEPTANCE CRITERIA

Project Acceptance Criteria sets the conditions for project delivery. It aligns
with the Client's need and Stakeholders' Expectations.
It's required to meet the Authority Requirements,
Codes, and Specifications.

TEMPLATE SUPPORT

Project Phase:

Initiation, Planning, Execution, Monitoring & Control, Closing

Deliverables:

Refer to WBS Package template in planning process group

Scope Statement:

Refer to Project Scope Statement in planning process group

Client's Need:

Fit-for-purpose, quality, safety, project completion time, budget, etc.

Code and Specifications:

Identify Industry Codes and Standards that are required to be followed in the project.
Identify the additional requirements beyond Standards and Codes, i.e., Project specifications.

Authorities Requirement:

Refer to the stakeholder analysis in Initiation process group and identify the relevant local or federal authorities and their requirement, which is necessary to get the approvals or NOCs from them.

Stakeholders' Expectation:

Refer to Stakeholder management template in Initiation process group.

Project Phase	Deliverables	Scope Statement	Client	Acceptance Criteria				
				Client's Need	Codes/Specifications	Authority Requirements	Stakeholder Expectations	Other

PROJECT MANAGEMENT

PROJECT RECOVERY PLAN

Project Recovery Plan is the document that provides the procedure to recover
the troubled project. This document identifies the delay activities
and finds out the root cause of the problem. It provides the
recovery strategy and corrective action to get
the project on track.

TEMPLATE SUPPORT

Project Phase:
___
Select the project phase that is affected. Project Phase: Initiation, Planning, Execution, Monitoring & Control, Closing

Project Deliverables:
___
List down the project deliverables that are affected. Concept Design Report, Preliminary Design Report, Detailed Design Report, Tender Documents, Cost Estimates, any other deliverables, etc.

Delay/Trouble Activities:
___
Identify the delay activities that trouble the project and are responsible for delay or loss in project. Type of delays: Delay in critical activities, delay in non-critical activities, excusable or non-excusable delay.

Real Impact:
___
Identify the real impact on the project due to trouble activities. Impact on cost, time, resources, communication, scope, etc.

Description:
___
Provide brief project scope and project background.

Root Cause:
___
Provide complete project assessment and identify the root cause of the project loss or delay. Following may be the root cause of delay: lack of resources, unidentified project scope, scope creep, delay in approvals, incomplete data, delay in data collection, team performance, project priority, unrealistic or tight project schedule, force majeure.

Recovery Strategy:
___
Provide project recovery strategy to get the project on track. Following techniques may apply: Schedule Compression that includes crashing, fast-tracking, and resource reallocation.

PROJECT RECOVERY PLAN

Client:	Date:
Project Title:	**Project No.:**

Project Phase:

- ☐ Initiation
- ☐ Planning
- ☐ Execution
- ☐ Monitoring & Control
- ☐ Closing

Project Deliverables:

- ☐
- ☐
- ☐
- ☐
- ☐

Delay/Trouble Activities:

- ☐
- ☐
- ☐
- ☐
- ☐

Real Impact:

- ☐ Cost
- ☐ Time
- ☐ Scope
- ☐ Resource
- ☐ Communication
- ☐ Others

Description:

Root Cause:

Recovery Strategy:

Corrective Action:

PROJECT RECOVERY PLAN

Project Phase	Deliverable / Milestone	Contractual Project Duration (Months)	Plan Start Date	Plan End Date	Actual Start Date	Actual End Date	Delay	Revised Duration as per Delay (Months)	Revised End Date	Recovery Duration (Months)

PROJECT MANAGEMENT

SCHEDULE OF SERVICES

Schedule of Services provides the planning of work assigned to a third party, sub-consultant, or sub-contractor. It defines third-party scope of work and duration of their tasks.

TEMPLATE SUPPORT

Third Party:

Sub-Consultant, Contractor, Vendor, or any other third party who is hired to perform the services that project team or organisation do not perform.

Brief Scope:

Prepare Scope of Work for third party. Define project boundary limit.

Duration:

Provide duration of service to third party to complete the assigned work.

Schedule Date:

Work Commencement date.

Delay:

Delay = (Actual End Date-Actual Start Date) – Planned duration

THIRD PARTY SCHEDULE OF SERVICES

Nos.	Third Party	Contact Name	Contact Number	Type of Work	Brief Scope	Duration	Schedule Date	Actual Start Date	Actual End Date	Delay

PROJECT MANAGEMENT

SCOPE RESPONSIBILTY MATRIX

Scope Responsibility Matrix refers to the document that identifies all the parties who carries out the project scope of work as a lead or support.

TEMPLATE SUPPORT

Scope Responsibility Matrix:

Sample Infrastructure project scope matrix
Project: Services for Road and Infrastructure Design.

Legend:
LEAD ●
SUPPORT ○

			SAMPLE SCOPE RESPOSIBILITY MATRIX			
No.	Scope of Work	Primary Consultant	Secondary Consultant	Sub-Consultant (Name)	Contractor	Other (Name)
1	Master Plan					●
2	Road Upgrade and Design	●				
3	Traffic Study	○		● (Name)		
4	Road Safety Audit			● (Name)		
5	Wet Utilities Design	●				
6	Geotechnical Study	○		● (Name)		
7	Power & Street Lighting	●				
8	Landscape	●				
9	Structure Design	●				
10	Firefighting	●				
11	Telecom	●				
12	Environmental Study	○		● (Name)		

CHAPTER 3
EXECUTION PROCESS

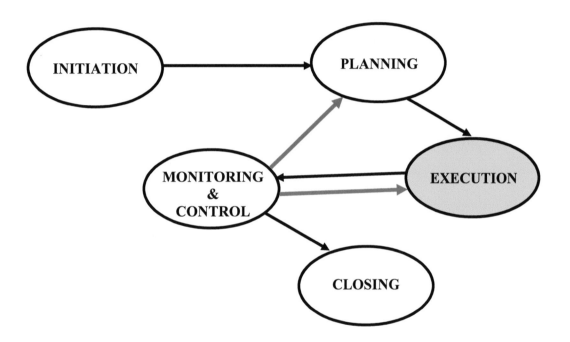

Execution is the process that is carried out in order to **complete** the
work specified in the **project management plan** in
order to meet the **project's requirements**.

PROJECT MANAGEMENT

LIST OF TEMPLATES AND FORMS

1. Project Status Report

2. Meeting Minutes

3. Change Order

4. Technical & Commercial Bid Evaluation

5. Comments Resolution Sheet

6. Technical Query Form

7. Site Visit Report

8. Issue Log

PROJECT MANAGEMENT

PROJECT STATUS REPORT

Project Status report provides the overall project status for
evaluation and project tracking. The report highlights the
progress of project costs and schedule.
Identify key risks and issues.

TEMPLATE SUPPORT

Project Scope:

Refer to Project Scope Statement and WBS Package template to define scope.

Safety and Quality Statistics:

Write any event that contains any safety and quality issues, like any injuries, near misses, causality, accuracy of data, accuracy of work, defects, and deficiency.

Key Contractual Dates:

Refer to Contract Agreement and Project Charter template.

Overall Project Progress Status:

- Status:
  Green-Project on track.

  Yellow-Project would need assistance.

  Red-Project is in trouble with serious issues.

- % weightage: based on the effort

PROJECT STATUS REPORT

CLIENT:

CLIENT AGREEMENT NO.:

PROJECT TITLE:

PROJECT SCOPE

SAFETY AND QUALITY STATISTICS (IF ANY)

KEY CONTRACTUAL DATES

✪ **Project Commencement Date:**

✪ **Project Completion Date:**

Stage	Milestone	Contractual Date	Actual Date	Delay
1.				
2.				
3.				
4.				
5.				
6.				
7.				

OVERALL PROJECT PROGRESS STATUS

✪ Project Progress – Overall

Description	Status		
Scope			
Schedule			
Cost			
Resources			

Stage	Milestone	Weightage (%)	Baseline		Variance (%)	Remarks
			Plan Progress (%)	Actual Progress (%)		

STATUS: ☐ ☐ ☐

☐

☐

☐

MAJOR ACTIVITIES COMPLETED FOR THE REPORTING PERIOD

☑

☑

☑

Deliverables Issued:

☑

☑

☑

Comments Received:

☑

☑

MEETINGS ATTENDED FOR THE REPORTING PERIOD

☑

☑

☑

SITE VISITS FOR THE REPORTING PERIOD

☑

☑

☑

ACTIVITIES PLANNED FOR NEXT PERIOD-LOOK AHEAD

☑

☑

☑

DELIVERABLE PENDING FOR COMMENTS / APPROVAL FROM CLIENT

☑

☑

☑

PENDING FROM CLIENT DEFICIENCY LIST

☑

☑

☑

Disciplines	Achievements This Period	Objectives for Next Period	Remarks (Concerns / Corrective actions)
General	✪ ✪ ✪	☑ ☑ ☑	
Discipline 1	✪ ✪ ✪	☑ ☑ ☑	
Discipline 2	✪ ✪ ✪	☑ ☑ ☑	
Discipline 3	✪ ✪ ✪	☑ ☑ ☑	
Discipline 4	✪ ✪ ✪	☑ ☑ ☑	
Others	✪ ✪ ✪	☑ ☑ ☑	

CORRESPONDENCE STATUS

Letters to Client:

Fax to Client:

Transmittals Issued to Client:

DETAILS OF TECHNICAL QUERIES

☑

☑

FINANCIAL STATUS

CONSULTANT PAYMENT STATUS				
Payment Milestones	Original Contract Amount	Invoiced Amount	To be Invoiced Amount	Paid Amount
TOTAL				

AREAS OF CONCERN / KEY RISKS

☑

☑

RECOMMENDED / REMEDIAL ACTIONS

☑

☑

PROJECT MANAGEMENT
MEETING MINUTES

Meeting report (Minutes of meeting) is the record of meeting proceedings.
It assigns the action items to be taken by individuals or any stakeholder.
It also provides the key information of the meeting subject.

TEMPLATE SUPPORT

Discussion:
_____

Record the conversation and action points.

Action By:
_____

- Company
- Client
- Stakeholders
- Any other meeting participant

Date	:
Venue	:
Subject	:
Issue date	:

External Attendees (Client & Major Stakeholders)	Company Attendees
Recorded By:	
Approved By _____	_____ Company Project Manager
Distribution:	
1. All attendees	
2.	

S/N	Discussion	Action By	Date

Meeting Attendance Register

Client:	
Project Title:	Project No.:
Topic:	Date:
Venue:	Time:

No.	Name	Designation	Company	Email ID	Signatures

PROJECT MANAGEMENT

CHANGE ORDER

Change Order is the document used for claiming any changes or any potential variation in the project.

TEMPLATE SUPPORT

Phase:

Initiation, Planning, Execution, Monitoring & Control, Closing

Potential Effect:

Cost, Time, Scope, Resource, Communication, Others

Reason for Change:

- Client
- Stakeholders
- Others

Variation:

- Design
- Quality
- Quantity
- Resources

Decision:

Approval

Rejection

Further information required

CHANGE ORDER
Potential Change in Project

Client:	Date:
Project Title:	Project No.:
Phase:	**Potential Effect:**
☐ Initiation ☐ Planning ☐ Execution ☐ Monitoring & Control ☐ Closing	☐ Cost: ☐ Time: ☐ Scope: ☐ Resource: ☐ Communication: ☐ Others
Reason for Change: ☐ ☐	**Variation:** ☐ Design: ☐ Quality: ☐ Quantity: ☐ Resources:

Description:
Justification:
Client /Third-Party Assessment:
Decision:

PROJECT MANAGEMENT

TECHNICAL & COMMERCIAL BID EVALUATION

Bid Evaluation is the process to examine the submitted bids and rank the bidders based on technical qualification and commercial price.
A successful bidder shall be awarded the contract.

TEMPLATE SUPPORT

Score:

% weightage =100

Average Score:

Achieved score based on % weightage

Description:

Evaluation Criteria

Technical Ranking:

Technical ranking based on total achieved points

Minimum Cut-off Points:

Minimum 50% required to qualify

Item/Services:

Services or material to be priced

Discounted %:

Bidder may provide further discount on original price.

Nos	Bid Technical Evaluation		Bidder 1	Bidder 2	Bidder 3
No	Description	Score	Average Score	Average Score	Average Score
1	Previous experience with company				
2	Similar experience with other companies				
3	Company capacity & experience, work in hand and work completed- last 5 years.				
4	Technical write-up and methodology				
5	Project staff organization chart including key personnel with C. Vs				
6	Company current workload				
7	Resources - Manpower				
8	Resources - List of Equipment				
9	Classification Certificate				
10	Commercial License				
11	Financial data (financial statements for past 3 years)				
12	HSEQ Certification (ISO 14001- OHSAS 18001- ISO 9001)				
13	Full compliance with the technical and commercial requirement of the Tender Documents without qualification or exclusion				
	Minimum Cut-off points	**50**			
	TOTAL SCORE	**100**			

SUMMARY		
Bidder Name	**Technical Ranking**	**Technical Points Achieved**
	1st	
	2nd	
	3rd	

	COMMERCIAL BID EVALUATION			
Nos	**Items /Services**	**Bidder -1**	**Bidder -2**	**Bidder -3**
		Amount	**Amount**	**Amount**
1				
2				
3				
4				
5				
6				
7				
8				
9				
10				
Total Amount				
Discounted %				
Discount Amount				
Final Value				

	SUMMARY			
Commercial Ranking Level	**Bidder**	**Commercial Offer**	**Technical Ranking**	**Technical Points Achieved**
1st				
2nd				
3rd				

PROJECT MANAGEMENT

COMMENTS RESOLUTION SHEET

Comments Resolution sheet is used for incorporating the comments
and providing a response to the comments raised by the
client or stakeholder.

TEMPLATE SUPPORT

Reviewer:
_____

Person who reviews the document or deliverable and provides comments

Reference Section:
_____

Section that has been reviewed and commented on

Company Response:
_____

Provide the answer or solution of open comments

Status:
_____

- Open
- Closed

COMMENTS RESOLUTION SHEET

Project Name:		Project Reference	
Status Code	Document No.	Revision No.	Document Title

No.	Reviewer	Reference Section	Comments Received	Company Response	Status (Closed-/ Open)

PROJECT MANAGEMENT

TECHNICAL QUERY FORM

Technical Query form is used to raise the question to the client or stakeholder for their recommendation and seek their acceptance for a proposed solution.

TEMPLATE SUPPORT

Project Reference:

Project Number or Client Agreement Number

Type of Query:

- Deviation
- Routine
- Urgent

Technical Query:

Question raised by consultant to the client

Clarifications-/ Recommendations

Clarifications-/recommendation received by client on technical query

TECHNICAL QUERY			
Project Reference	**Project Title**		**Query No:**
	Client:	Location:	Date:

Type of query
☐ **Deviation**
☐ **Routine**
☐ **Urgent**

Subject:	Discipline:

Technical query

Proposed Solution (s):

RAISED BY:	DESIGNATION:	SIGNATURE:

CLARIFICATIONS/ RECOMMENDATIONS

Proposed Solution acceptable	☐ Yes ☐ No	☐ Refer to response below

CLEARED BY:	SIGNATURE:	DATE:

PROJECT MANAGEMENT

SITE VISIT REPORT

Site Visit report documents the on-site progress. It provides the site data and highlights the site condition.

TEMPLATE SUPPORT

Project Background:

Provide a common description of the project.

Project Objective:

Fit-for-purpose, quality, safety, project completion time, budget, and any other

Purpose of the Document:

To record the information of the site visit

Site Visit Objective:

Purpose and need of site visit

Site Visit Attendance:

List the personnel name and their organization who visits the site.

Site Visit Observations:

Record the site condition.

Data Collection:

Gathering the site data

Site Visit Report

Project Background:

Project Objective:

Purpose of the Document:

Site Visit Objective:

Site Visit Attendance:

Site visit date:

Location:

SITE VISIT ATTENDANCE

Sr. No.	Discipline/Designation	Organisation	Key Personnel

Site Visit Observations:

Data Collection:

Summary:

Conclusion:

Site Photographs:

PROJECT MANAGEMENT

ISSUE LOG

Issue Log is the list of difficulties and problems that arise during all phases of the project.

TEMPLATE SUPPORT

Project Phase:
Initiation, Planning, Execution, Monitoring& Control, Closing

Issue Type:
- General
- Technical

Owner:
Team member who takes ownership of the issue and will be accountable

Issue Priority:
- High
- Medium
- Low
- Negligible

Impact:

- Cost
- Time
- Quality
- Resources
- Communication
- Scope
- Others

Solution:

Provide mitigation measure to solve the issue.

ISSUE LOG										
Issue ID	Project Phase	Issue Type	Description	Owner	Issue Priority	Impact	Solution	Date Identified	Target Date	Date Resolved

CHAPTER 4
MONITORING & CONTROL PROCESS

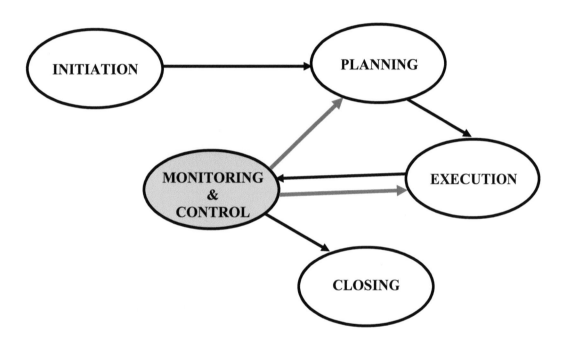

Monitoring & Control is the process that is necessary to **monitor, review**, and **control** the project's **progress** and **performance**; recognize any areas where **improvements** to the plan are required; and implement those changes.

PROJECT MANAGEMENT

MONITORING & CONTROL

LIST OF TEMPLATES AND FORMS

1. Risk Breakdown Structure

2. Risk Register

3. Earn Value Analysis

4. S-Curve

5. Project Audit Report

6. Non-Conformity Report

7. Inspection Form

PROJECT MANAGEMENT

RISK BREAKDOWN STRUCTURE

Risk Breakdown Structure is a hierarchical representation of Risk.
Risk categories are defined on different levels.

TEMPLATE SUPPORT

Risk Breakdown Structure:

Sample Risk Breakdown Structure of Infrastructure Design Project

Risk Categories:

Level 0

Level 1

Level 2

Level 3

PROJECT						
External Risk	Communication	Tender Process	Procurement	Design	Project Management	Construction
Client	Internal	Pre-tender stage	Supplier Risk	Design Method	Scope	Site Condition
Contractor	External	Tender Stage	Material	Design Assumption	Time	Construction Procedure
Stakeholders	Information	Evaluation Stage	Change in material price	Design Delay	Cost	Construction Occupational Safety
	Project Admin	Contract Award Stage	Equipment	Quality	Quality	Quality
			Make & Buy Analysis		Human Resource	
					Project Management Plans	
					Project Priorities	

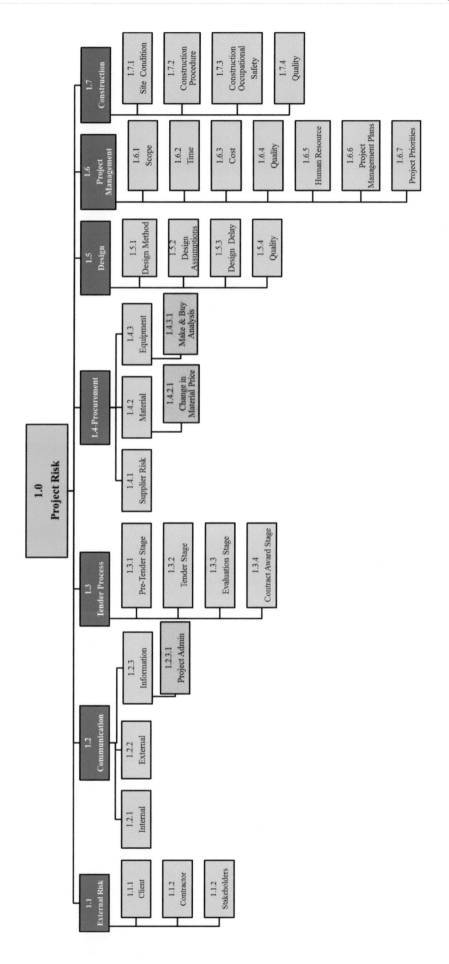

PROJECT MANAGEMENT

RISK REGISTER

Risk Register is a Risk Management tool to identify the potential risks. Analyze
the risks and identify the risk level based on risk severity.
Risk Register also provides the Risk
Response and Mitigation.

TEMPLATE SUPPORT

QUALITATIVE RISK ANALYSIS
MATRIX AND SCORING

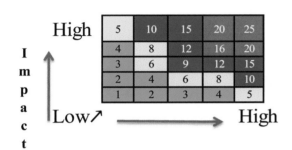

RISK LEVEL	
Risk	**Score**
Low	1-4
Moderate	5-8
High	9-15
Extreme	16-25

Probability

Risk Score=Probability X Impact

Risk Response Strategy for Opportunity & Threat:

- Avoid (Threat)
- Mitigate (Threat)
- Transfer (Threat)
- Exploit (Opportunity)
- Enhance (Opportunity)
- Share (Opportunity)
- Accept (Opportunity & Threat)

Risk Type:

- Internal
- External

Risk Category:

- Project Management
- Design
- Construction
- Communication
- Organizational
- OHSE
- Financial
- Contractual
- Document Control

Risk Level:

- Extreme
- High
- Medium
- Low

Risk Score:

Risk Score = Probability x Impact

Risk Priority:

Define priority based on Risk Score.

Risk Mitigation:

Remove or reduce the impact of risk.

Trigger:

Warning sign or symptom of risk event

Risk Owner:

Project team member responsible and accountable to control the risk

RISK IDENTIFICATION					RISK ANALYSIS					RISK MANAGEMENT						
Risk ID	Risk Description	Risk Category	Risk Cause	Risk Type	Risk Status (Active /Close)	Probability	Impact	Score	Risk Level	Risk Priority	Risk Response	Mitigation	Trigger	Risk Owner	Review Date	Days Over Due	Risk Close Date

PROJECT
MANAGEMENT

EARN VALUE ANALYSIS

Earn Value Analysis is the tool to measure the project progress. It provides the forecast and actual status of the project. This tool gives the review of the schedule and cost of the project.

TEMPLATE SUPPORT

Earn Value Matrix:

- PV- Budgeted Cost of Work Scheduled (Planned Value)
- EV- Budgeted Cost of Work Performed (Earned Value)
- AC- Actual Cost of Work Performed (Cost)
- CV- Cost Variance
- SV -Schedule Variance
- CPI -Cost Performance Index
- SPI- Schedule Performance Index
- EAC -Estimate at Completion
- BAC- Budget at Completion
- ETC- Estimate to Complete the Project
- VAC- Variance at Completion

Project Status:

SPI-Schedule Performance Index

SPI=EV / PV

- SPI < 1 – Project is behind schedule
- SPI = 1 – Project is on schedule
- SPI > 1-Project is ahead of schedule

CPI-Cost Performance Index

CPI=EV / AC

- CPI < 1 – Project is performing with profit
- CPI = 1 – Project is on budget
- CPI > 1-Project is performing at loss

Cost Variance:

$$\text{Cost Variance (CV)} = \text{Earn Value (EV)} - \text{Actual Cost (AC)}$$

- Project is under budget if the Cost Variance is positive.
- Project is over budget if the Cost Variance is negative.
- Project is on budget if the Cost Variance is zero.

Schedule Variance:

$$\text{Schedule Variance} = \text{Earn Value (EV)} - \text{Planned Value (PV)}$$

- Project is ahead of schedule if the Schedule Variance is positive.
- Project is behind schedule if the Schedule Variance is negative.
- Project is on schedule if the Schedule Variance is zero.

% Project Completion:

Actual Cost / Budget at Completion = AC / BAC

Confidence Level:

Range 0 % to 100%

Physical Completion:

Actual % completion of work at reporting period time

Earn Value (EV):

EV= BAC x Confidence level (%) x % physical completion

Remaining Hours:

Remaining hours (planned) to complete the work

Actual Hours Spent:

Actual hours consumed at reporting period time

Actual Cost Spent (AC):

Actual cost spent from overall budget (BAC) at reporting period time

Planned Value (PV):

Budgeted cost of work scheduled = BAC x Planned % of complete

Estimate at Completion (EAC):

EAC = BAC / CPI or AC +ETC or AC + (BAC-EV)

Estimate to complete the project (ETC):

EAC = EAC - AC

Variance at Completion (VAC):

VAC = BAC – EAC

Serial No.	Project Data	Equation/Input	January	February	March	April	May	June	July	August	September	October	November	December
A	Budget Hours													
B	Budget Cost (BAC)													
C	% Completion (Cost Spent)	AC / BAC												
D	Confidence Level (%)													
E	Physical Completion (%)													
F	Earned Value (EV)	B X D X E												
G	Remaining Hours to Complete													
H	Actual Hours Spent													
I	Actual Cost Spent (AC)													
J	Planned Value (PV)	BAC X Planned % complete												
K	Cost Variance (CV)	EV-AC												
L	Cost Performance Index (CPI)	EV/AC												
M	Estimate at Completion (EAC)	BAC / CPI												
N	Estimate to Completion (ETC)	EAC-AC												
O	Variance at Completion (VAC)	BAC-EAC												
P	Schedule Performance Index (SPI)	EV / PV												
Q	Schedule Variance (SV)	EV-PV												
R	Budget Status													
S	Schedule Status													

PROJECT MANAGEMENT

S-CURVE

S-Curve is the graphical representation of cumulative cost against project duration. S-Curve is used to measure the project performance.

TEMPLATE SUPPORT

S-Curve Calculation:

Series of Duration: Split the duration and draw the line on the bar chart where activity starts and ends.

Activity	Planned Duration (Days)	Series of Duration	Cost /Day	Series Duration Total Cost	Series Cumulative Cost
A	2	**1** (A-2 days)	300	300+300 =600	600
B	3	**2** (B-3 days)	400	400+400+400 =1200	600+1200 =1800
C	3	**3** (C-2 days, D-2 days)	400	(400+400) + (200+200) =1200	1200+1800 =3000
D	2	**4** (C-1 day, E-1 day)	200	(400) +(100) =500	500+3000 =3500
E	3	**5** (E-2 days)	100	100+100 =200	200+3500 =3700

Activity	Actual Duration (Days)	Series of Duration	Cost /Day	Series Duration Total Cost	Series Cumulative Cost
A	3	**1** (A-3 days)	300	300+300+300 =900	900
B	3	**2** (B-3 days)	400	400+400+400 =1200	900+1200 =2100
C	3	**3** (C-2 days, D-2 days)	400	(400+400) + (200+200) =1200	1200+2100 =3300
D	2	**4** (C-1 day, E-1 day)	200	(400) +(100) =500	500+3300 =3800
E	2	**5** (E-1 days)	100	100 =100	100+3800 =3900

S-Curve

Planned ⸺⸺⸺

Actual ⸻⸻⸻

SAMPLE S-CURVE

Activity	Predecessor	Planned Duration (Days)	Actual Duration (Days)	Cost/day (USD)
A	-	2	3	300
B	A	3	3	400
C	B	3	3	400
D	B	2	2	200
E	D	3	2	100

Planned Series of Duration

	1	2	3	4	5
Duration Total Cost	600	1200	1200	500	200
Cumulative Cost	600	1800	3000	3500	3700

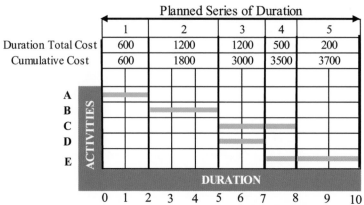

Actual Series of Duration

	1	2	3	4	5
Duration Total Cost	900	1200	1200	500	100
Cumulative Cost	900	2100	3300	3800	3900

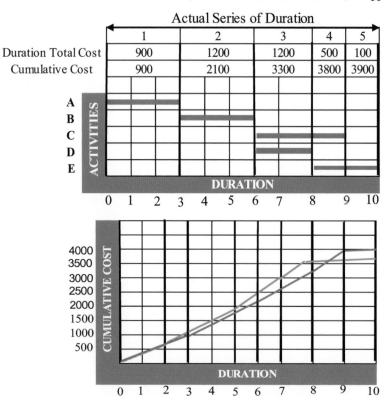

PROJECT MANAGEMENT
INTERNAL AUDIT REPORT

Internal Audit report is the review of the project. Find the deviations from standards and requirements. Review compliance with the statement of work. Identify the nonconformity and observations.

TEMPLATE SUPPORT

Internal Auditor:

Independent person who evaluates and reviews the project processes

Name of Auditees:

Project Team members who are being audited

Standard to follow:

ISO latest standards

Object-/Purpose of Audit:

Identify the problems, deviations, and issues to improve the project process.

Audit Scope:

Set the project audit boundaries--who, what, when, where?

Audit Reference Document:

ISO standard, Project-specific standard and specifications, Project Management Plan, Contract Agreement, Others

Audit Samples and Evidence:

Documents or process that are being checked during audit--reports, drawings, project documents, financial documents, others

Nonconformity:

Deviation from standard or reference document. Nonconformity has to be properly closed. Refer to the nonconformity report.

Observations:

Observations are minor findings that can be or cannot be closed.

PROJECT AUDIT

Audit Number:

Audit Date:

Location:

Internal Auditor:
Auditor(s):

Name of Auditees:

Standard to Follow: Latest ISO Standards

Objective / Purpose of Audit

Audit Scope

Reference Documents

Departments to be Audited

Audit Samples and Evidence

Nonconformity /Findings		
NCR ID:	Reference	Description

Observations		
Observation No:	Minor/Major	Description

PROJECT MANAGEMENT

NCR REPORT

Nonconformity report (NCR) addresses the deviations and the root cause of the nonconformity. It provides the corrective actions and the implementation strategy.

TEMPLATE SUPPORT

Findings:

Defect or deviation observed during project audit.

Auditees:

Project Team members who are being audited.

Cause Analysis:

Method of problem solving for identifying the cause of defects and deviations

Correction & Corrective Action:

Take appropriate actions and steps to fix the defects.

Implementation & Review:

Review & Implement the corrective actions.

Status:

Open, Closed

No.	NCR ID	Auditees	Findings	Cause Analysis	Corrective Action	Implementation & Review	Status	Remarks

PROJECT
MANAGEMENT
INSPECTION FORM

Inspection is to provide the assessment of the system or condition of the product
and element. Identify the defect and its cause and provide
mitigation measures.

TEMPLATE SUPPORT

Element:

Material, equipment, any physical item

Type of Defects:

Physical defect
Quality defect
Design defect
Process defect

Condition:

Good
Bad

Action Required:

Action required to fix the defect

Expected Cost:

Cost to fix the defect

INSPECTION FORM								
ID No.	Element	Description	(Type of Defect)	Cause of Defect	Condition		Action Required	Expected Cost
					Good	Bad		

CHAPTER 5
CLOSING PROCESS

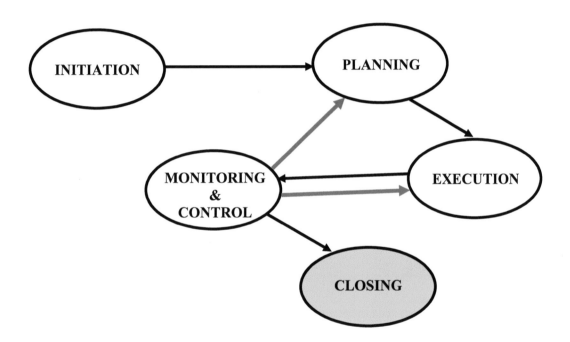

Closing is the process that is carried out to formally **complete** or close the **project, phase**, or **contract.**

PROJECT MANAGEMENT

CLOSING

LIST OF TEMPLATES AND FORMS

1.Project Post-Mortem Report

2.Project Close-out Form

3.Lesson Learned

4.Project Team Performance Evaluation

PROJECT MANAGEMENT

PROJECT POST-MORTEM REPORT

Project Post-Mortem report provides the success and failure of the project. Examine the project challenges and requirements.

TEMPLATE SUPPORT

Project Post-Mortem Questions:

Answer the questions about the project's success and failure.

Summary and Recommendations:

Provide the overall performance of the project.

	PROJECT POST MORTEM REPORT		
	Post-Mortem Questions	**Comments**	**Answer/ Additional Comments**
1	How clearly defined was the Scope for this project?	Very, somewhat, not very, not at all	
2	What was the bottleneck of your project?	Provide Detail	
3	Was project budget well-defined?	Yes, No	
4	Was customer satisfied with the product?	Yes, No	
5	Were project objectives met?	Yes, No	
6	What were the main sources of frustration in the project?	Provide Detail	
7	Which stage took more time than scheduled?	Provide Name	
8	What were up to five main causes for schedule slips, and how could we avoid those causes in the future?	Provide Detail	
9	How many times did team members rework due to correction or not clearly understanding the scope of work?	Provide Detail	
10	How efficient and effective were the project team?	Very, somewhat, not very, not at all	
11	How efficient and effective were technical meetings?	Very, somewhat, not very, not at all	
12	How efficient and effective were client meetings?	Very, somewhat, not very, not at all	
13	How efficient and effective were project team meetings?	Very, somewhat, not very, not at all	
14	How well did top management support this project?	Very, somewhat, not very, not at all	
15	Was the team appreciated and recognized for efforts?	Yes, No	
16	How was the Project Manager role as a Leader on this project?	Provide Detail	
17	What was the Leadership style during the project?	Facilitator, Forcing, Directing, Consultative	
18	How clear were you on your role in the project as a Project Manager?	Very, somewhat, not very, not at all	
19	Was the client satisfied with the information they received?	Yes, No	
20	How many revisions were done for Deliverables?	Provide Detail	
21	How effective were our design reviews?	Very, somewhat, not very, not at all	
22	How effective was our design based on the client's review?	Very, somewhat, not very, not at all	
23	How effective and quick was client response on reports?	Very, somewhat, not very, not at all	
24	How effective was client response on issues?	Very, somewhat, not very, not at all	

	PROJECT POST-MORTEM REPORT		
	Post-Mortem Questions	**Comments**	**Answer/ Additional Comments**
25	How effective was interaction/cooperation between contractor, client, and company office?	Very, somewhat, not very, not at all	
26	Were requirements or data gathered to sufficient detail?	Yes, No	
27	Was the project team properly organized and staffed?	Yes, No	
28	Were requirements documented clearly?	Yes, No	
29	How was delay controlled?	Provide Detail	
30	Which department was involved in delaying to produce the deliverable?	Name of the Department and Reason	
31	Any delays in invoicing and receiving the payment from client?	Provide Detail	
32	Were tasks defined adequately?	Yes, No	
33	Were the customer's needs/requirements met?	Yes, No	
34	Was the project plan and schedule well-documented, with appropriate structure and detail?	Yes, No	
35	Were design or any other changes in scope well-controlled?	Yes, No	
36	How was the team commitment?	Very, somewhat, not very, not at all	
37	How was coordination between different disciplines?	Very, somewhat, not very, not at all	
38	How did you resolve problems and issues with the client, contractor, & PM Team?	Forcing, problem, smoothing, (win-win) solving, compromising, withdrawal, Provide Detail	
	Summary and Recommendations		
1	Performance against Goals		
2	Performance against Schedule		
3	Performance against Quality		
4	Performance against Budget or Cost		
5	How smooth project was completed as per scope and client requirement		
6	What went right?		
7	What went wrong?		
8	Key Areas of Improvement		
9	For the next project, how/ what could we improve in the way the project was conducted?		

PROJECT MANAGEMENT

PROJECT CLOSE-OUT REPORT

Project Close-out report uses for official closure of the project. Report provides the summary of the project. It is required to archive the project.

TEMPLATE SUPPORT

Project Title:

Name of the Project in the contract assigned by client

Project Manager:

Name the project manager of the company who is assigned to the project.

Type of Contract:

- Reimbursable
- Lump sum
- Design-built
- Joint venture
- Other

PROJECT CLOSE-OUT REPORT

Project Title:

Client:

Project Manager:

Type of Contract:

Nos.	Checklist	Response
1.	Project Start Date	
2.	Project End Date	
3.	Contract Duration	
4.	Time Extension	
5.	Revised Contract Duration	
6.	Contract Budget	
7.	Variation Order (Cost)	
8.	Revised Budget	
9.	Project Overrun (Cost)	
10.	Profit /Loss	
11.	All Invoices Raised	
12.	All Payment Received	
13.	All Invoices Paid to Third Party	
14.	Client Acceptance Received	
15.	Project Final closeout review meeting with Management	
16.	Project Team Demobilized	
17.	Resources Released	
18.	Lesson Learned Submitted	
19.	Project Quality Audit	
20.	Bank Guarantees Returned from Client	
21.	Project Archived	

PROJECT MANAGEMENT

LESSON LEARNED REPORT

Lesson Learned provides the information about the project failure and success. It describes "what went right" and "what went wrong" in the project. Lesson Learned report is used for future projects to avoid mistakes and improve the process for future projects.

TEMPLATE SUPPORT

Category:

- Project integration management
- Project scope management
- Project time management
- Project cost management
- Project quality management
- Project resource management
- Project communications management
- Project risk management

Type of Contract:

- Reimbursable
- Lump sum
- Design-built
- Joint venture
- Other

Impact:

Cost, Time, Quality, Scope, Resources, Communication, Other

LESSON LEARNED

Project Title:

Project Manager:

Type of Contract:

No.	Category	Observation	Cause	Impact	Resolution

PROJECT MANAGEMENT

PROJECT TEAM PERFORMANCE EVALUATION

Project Team Performance evaluation identifies the strength and weakness of each project team member. This will help to improve weaknesses and provide the opportunity to develop skills.

TEMPLATE SUPPORT

Assessment Criteria:

Competency-based assessment

Performance Rating Scale:

This is a 5-point performance rating scale

- 5– Outstanding
- 4– Exceeds Expectations
- 3- Meets Expectations
- 2- Needs Improvement
- 1- Unacceptable

Nos.	Assessment Criteria	Performance Rating Scale				
		1	2	3	4	5
Team Member Name:						
1	Project Understanding					
2	Project Scope Understanding					
3	Understand Client's Need					
4	Technical Capabilities					
5	Communication					
6	Team Work					
7	Punctuality					
8	Task Ownership					
9	Meeting Task Deadline					
10	Leadership Quality					
11	Quality Work					
12	Innovation					
13	Results-Oriented					
14	Adaptability					
15	Project Priority Setting					
16	Stress Control					

PROJECT TEAM PERFORMANCE EVALUATION

Printed in Great Britain
by Amazon

21733211R10107